by
Chelsey Luciow

CAPSTONE PRESS
a capstone imprint

Dabble Lab is published by Capstone Press, an imprint of Capstone.
1710 Roe Crest Drive, North Mankato, Minnesota 56003
capstonepub.com

Copyright © 2025 by Capstone. All rights reserved. No part of this publication may be reproduced in whole or in part, or stored in a retrieval system, or transmitted in any form or by any means, electronic, mechanical, photocopying, recording, or otherwise, without written permission of the publisher.

Library of Congress Cataloging-in-Publication Data is available on the Library of Congress website.
ISBN: 9781669093077 (hardcover)
ISBN: 9781669093039 (ebook PDF)

Summary: Get a taste of the world when you cook up lunch across cultures! From Peruvian avocado sandwiches to Finnish fish soup to Egyptian cucumber salad, these easy-to-make recipes are sure to make your afternoon brighter.

Image Credits: Adobe Stock: donatas1205, 28 (background), Obsessively (background), 12, 16, 20, 27, Sharmin, 19 (background); Shutterstock: Brent Hofacker, 31; Mighty Media, Inc. (project photos)
Design Elements: Adobe Stock: byMechul, zhaluldesign; Mighty Media, Inc.

Editorial Credits
Editor: Jessica Rusick
Designer: Denise Hamernik

Any additional websites and resources referenced in this book are not maintained, authorized, or sponsored by Capstone. All product and company names are trademarks™ or registered® trademarks of their respective holders.

The publisher and the author shall not be liable for any damages allegedly arising from the information in this book, and they specifically disclaim any liability from the use or application of any of the contents of this book.

Table of Contents

Cooking Up Lunch 4
Peruvian Triple Sandwiches 6
Nigerian Bean Porridge 9
Greek Salad with Orzo 10
Chinese Scissor-Cut Noodles 13
Italian Caprese Salad 14
Egyptian Cucumber and Tomato Salad 17
French Onion Soup 18
Fijian Palusami 21
Finnish Salmon Soup 22
Indian Cucumber Pancakes 25
Colombian Bocadillo con Queso 26
Polish Pierogi 29
Hawaiian SPAM Musubi 30

    Read More 32
    Internet Sites 32
    About the Author 32

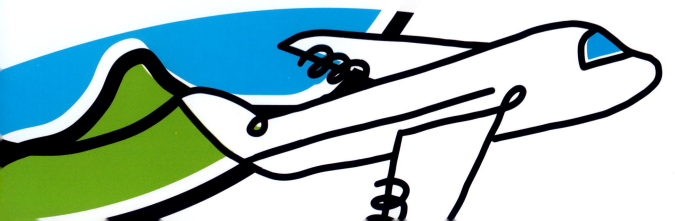

Cooking Up
LUNCH

In some cultures, lunch is seen as the day's main meal. In many other cultures, lunch is a lighter meal featuring dishes such as sandwiches, soups, and salads. Kids in countries around the world eat all kinds of lunch food! Many meals are beloved dishes in the cultures they come from. Make a Greek salad, French onion soup, Nigerian bean porridge, and more to experience foods from many cultures!

Basic Supplies

- aluminum foil
- baking sheet
- colander
- frying pan
- grater
- juicer
- knife and cutting board
- measuring cups and spoons
- mixing bowls
- spatula
- whisk

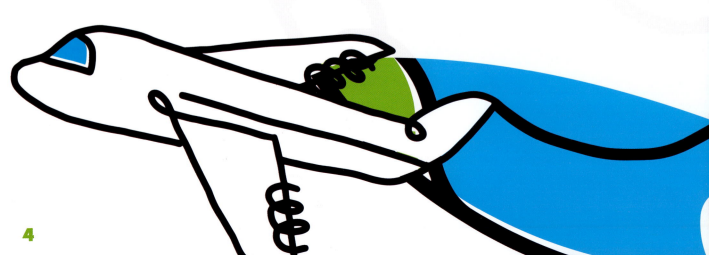

Kitchen Tips

1. Ask an adult for permission before you make a recipe.

2. Ask an adult for help when using a knife, blender, grater, stove, or oven. Wear oven mitts when removing items from the oven or microwave.

3. Read through the recipe and set out all ingredients and supplies before you start working.

4. Using metric tools? Use the conversion chart on the right to make your recipe measure up.

5. Wash your hands before and after you handle food. Wash and dry fresh produce before use.

6. When you are done making food, clean your work surface and wash dirty dishes. Put all supplies and ingredients back where you found them.

Standard	Metric
¼ teaspoon	1.25 grams or milliliters
½ teaspoon	2.5 g or mL
1 teaspoon	5 g or mL
1 tablespoon	15 g or mL
¼ cup	57 g (dry) or 60 mL (liquid)
⅓ cup	75 g (dry) or 80 mL (liquid)
½ cup	114 g (dry) or 125 mL (liquid)
⅓ cup	150 g (dry) or 160 mL (liquid)
¾ cup	170 g (dry) or 175 mL (liquid)
1 cup	227 g (dry) or 240 mL (liquid)
1 quart	950 mL

Peruvian Triple Sandwiches

This is a favorite finger sandwich at gatherings in Peru. Many Peruvians consider it a comforting and easy lunch.

Ingredients
(makes 8 small sandwiches)

- 1 ripe avocado
- ¼ teaspoon lime juice
- salt and pepper to taste
- 1 tomato, sliced
- 1 hard-boiled egg, sliced
- mayonnaise
- 8 slices white bread, crusts removed

1. Cut the avocado in half. Remove the pit. Cut the flesh into slices while it is still in the peel. Use a spoon to scoop the slices into a small bowl. Sprinkle the lime juice and salt and pepper over the slices. Set the bowl aside.

2. Sprinkle the tomato slices and hard-boiled egg slices with salt and pepper.

3. Assemble a sandwich. Spread mayonnaise on one side of a bread slice. Layer half the avocado slices on top.

4. Spread mayonnaise on both sides of a second bread slice. Place it on top of the avocado. Layer half the tomato slices on top.

5. Spread mayonnaise on both sides of a third bread slice. Lay it on top of the tomato. Layer half the egg slices on top.

6. Spread mayonnaise on one side of a fourth bread slice and lay it on top of the egg.

7. Repeat steps 3 through 6 to build a second sandwich.

8. Cut each sandwich into four parts. Eat the sandwiches yourself or share them!

Three Parts

Spanish is Peru's official language. In Spanish, *triple* (TREE-play) means "having three parts." The triple sandwich is named for its three main ingredients: avocado, tomato, and egg.

7

Stirred Beans

Yoruba is one of Nigeria's main languages. The Yoruba name for bean porridge is *ewa riro* (eh-WAH REE-roh), which means "stirred beans."

Nigerian Bean Porridge

Nigeria grows most of the world's black-eyed peas, which are a kind of bean. They are a major source of protein in Nigerian diets.

Ingredients
(makes 4 servings)

- 15-ounce can black-eyed peas
- 2 tablespoons vegetable oil
- 1 onion, chopped
- 2 garlic cloves, minced
- 2 tomatoes, chopped
- ⅛ teaspoon cayenne pepper (optional)
- 1 teaspoon paprika
- salt and pepper to taste

1. Rinse the black-eyed peas thoroughly in a colander. Set them aside.
2. Heat the oil in a pot over medium-high heat. Put the onion and garlic in the pot and cook until soft and fragrant.
3. Add the tomatoes to the pot. Lower the heat to medium. Let the tomatoes simmer until they are soft and release their juices.
4. Add the cayenne pepper (if using), paprika, and drained beans to the pot. Stir the mixture.
5. Cover the pot and turn the heat to low. Let the mixture simmer for 10 minutes.
6. Taste the bean porridge and season with salt and pepper as desired.

Greek Salad with Orzo

Greek salad is made of vegetables and herbs traditional to Greek farmers. Though not traditional to Greek salad, orzo is used in many other Greek dishes.

Ingredients
(makes 4 servings)

- 1½ cups dry orzo pasta
- 1 pint cherry tomatoes, halved
- 2 green onions, chopped
- ½ green bell pepper, chopped
- 1 cup fresh parsley, chopped
- ½ cup fresh dill, chopped, plus extra
- ½ cup pitted kalamata olives, sliced
- 2 teaspoons capers
- 1 lemon, zested and juiced
- ¼ cup olive oil
- 1 garlic clove, minced
- 1 teaspoon dried oregano
- salt and pepper to taste
- ¼ cup crumbled feta cheese

1. Cook and drain the orzo according to the package's directions. Set the orzo aside.
2. Stir together the tomatoes, green onion, bell pepper, parsley, dill, olives, and capers in a large mixing bowl.
3. Add the cooked orzo to the bowl and stir the salad.
4. Make the dressing. Whisk together the lemon zest, lemon juice, olive oil, garlic, and oregano in a small bowl. Add salt and pepper to taste.
5. Drizzle the dressing over the salad. Stir until the salad is well-coated with dressing.
6. Top the salad with feta cheese. Cover and refrigerate the salad for at least 30 minutes before serving. Garnish with dill if you'd like.

Little Barley
In Greece, orzo is called *krithiraki* (KREE-tha-rah-kee), which means "little barley." That's because the shape of the pasta resembles that of a barley grain.

Language Lesson

In Mandarin Chinese, scissor-cut noodles are called *dao xiao mian* (DOW ZHOW me-EHN).

Chinese Scissor-Cut Noodles

These noodles are a common Chinese street food. Skilled chefs can cut nearly two hundred noodles in one minute!

Ingredients
(makes 4 servings)

- 3¾ cups white flour
- 1 teaspoon salt
- 1¼ cups water
- 6 tablespoons vegetable oil
- 1 green onion, minced
- 2 cloves of garlic, minced
- 2 teaspoons sesame seeds
- ½ teaspoon cayenne pepper
- 2 tablespoons soy sauce
- 1 tablespoon balsamic vinegar
- 1 cup baby spinach

1. Mix the flour and salt in a bowl. Add the water. Knead the mixture until it forms a smooth ball of dough. Cover the dough with a clean dish cloth. Let it rest at room temperature for 15 minutes.

2. Bring a large pot of water to a gentle boil.

3. Cut the dough into quarters. Shape each quarter into a patty ¾ inches (1.9 centimeters) thick.

4. Hold a patty over the pot of water. Use kitchen scissors to cut noodle strips off of it. Each noodle should be about 2 inches (5 cm) long and ¼ inch (0.6 cm) wide. Let the noodles drop into the water. Repeat with each patty.

5. Cook the noodles for 6 minutes. Drain them in a colander.

6. Make the sauce. Heat the oil in a pan over medium-high heat. Add the green onion, garlic, sesame seeds, cayenne pepper, soy sauce, and vinegar. Stir until the sauce is warm and bubbling.

7. Add the noodles and spinach to the sauce. Stir until the noodles are coated and the spinach is wilted. Serve immediately.

Italian Caprese Salad

An Italian man invented caprese (kah-PRAY-zay) salad as a tribute to Italy. The salad's colors (red, white, and green) represent the Italian flag.

Ingredients
(makes 4 servings)

- 2 tomatoes, sliced
- salt to taste
- 12 fresh basil leaves
- 8 ounces fresh mozzarella log, sliced
- 2 tablespoons balsamic vinegar glaze
- 2 tablespoons olive oil
- pepper to taste

1. Lay three tomato slices on a plate. Sprinkle them with salt to taste.
2. Wash the basil leaves in cold water. Lay three leaves in your palm. Slap your other palm on top of the leaves. This will help release the basil's flavor.
3. Place one basil leaf on top of each tomato slice.
4. Lay one slice of mozzarella on top of each basil leaf.
5. Drizzle about ½ tablespoon vinegar glaze and ½ tablespoon olive oil over the salad. Top with pepper to taste.
6. Repeat steps 1 through 5 to make additional caprese salads.

Learn Lingo
"Lunch" in Italian is *pranzo* (PRAHN-zoh). *Buon appetito* (BWOHN ah peh-TEE-toh) means "enjoy your meal."

Egyptian Cucumber and Tomato Salad

This salad is the national salad of Egypt. It celebrates Egypt's fresh produce and is served in homes, markets, and at festivals.

Ingredients
(makes 4 servings)

- 2 English cucumbers, diced
- 4 tomatoes, diced
- 1 bunch fresh Italian parsley, chopped
- 1 tablespoon vinegar
- juice of ½ lime
- 1 teaspoon salt
- ½ teaspoon pepper
- 1 tablespoon dried mint
- 1 small red onion, diced

1. Mix together the cucumbers, tomatoes, and parsley in a large bowl.
2. Add the vinegar, lime juice, salt, pepper, mint, and red onion to the bowl. Toss the salad together until everything is well coated.
3. Taste the salad and add more salt and pepper if desired. Serve the salad right away.

Salata Baladi

Egyptian salad is called *salata baladi* (sah-LAH-tah bah-LAH-dee) in Arabic. This translates to "country salad" or "traditional salad."

French Onion Soup

This soup has been a French favorite since the 1700s. It is commonly eaten on New Year's Eve.

Ingredients
(makes 6 servings)

- ¼ cup butter
- 4 white onions, thinly sliced
- 1 garlic clove, minced
- 6 cups water
- 8 beef bouillon cubes
- ¼ teaspoon salt
- ⅛ teaspoon black pepper
- 1 bay leaf
- 1 tablespoon Worcestershire sauce
- 1 loaf French bread
- 6-ounce block Gruyère cheese, shredded

1. Melt the butter in a pot over medium-high heat. Add the onion and cook until golden, about 5 to 10 minutes. Add the garlic and cook the mixture for another minute.

2. Add the water, bouillon cubes, salt, pepper, bay leaf, and Worcestershire sauce to the pot. Bring the mixture to a boil over high heat.

3. Cover the pot and lower the heat to medium. Let the soup simmer for 25 minutes, stirring occasionally.

4. While the soup simmers, preheat the oven to 350 degrees Fahrenheit (180 degrees Celsius). Cut the bread into slices and place them on a baking sheet. Sprinkle cheese on each slice.

5. Toast the bread in the oven for 5 minutes. Serve each bowl of soup with a slice of bread on top.

Kingly Soup
French onion soup is called *soupe à l'ognion* (SOOP ah loh-NYOH) in French. One legend claims that French king Louis XV invented it!

Three Languages

Fiji has three official languages: English, Fijian, and Fiji Hindi. Fijian is most people's first language. "Hello" in Fijian is *bula* (mbooh-lah). "Coconut" is *bu* (mboo).

Fijian Palusami

Palusami (pah-loo-SAH-me) dates to Fiji's Polynesian settlers. The dish traditionally has a coconut and onion filling. Modern versions include corned beef.

Ingredients
(makes 8 servings)

- 1 yellow onion, diced
- 2 cloves garlic, minced
- 14-ounce can corned beef hash
- 1 teaspoon salt
- ½ teaspoon pepper
- 2 bunches Swiss chard
- 13.5-ounce can coconut cream

1. Preheat the oven to 350°F (180°C).
2. Mix together the onion, garlic, corned beef, salt, and pepper in a bowl. This is the filling.
3. Cut the stems off the Swiss chard leaves.
4. Cut a sheet of aluminum foil large enough to wrap around a leaf. Stack two leaves in the center of the foil.
5. Spoon 3 tablespoons of filling in the center of the stacked leaves. Drizzle 1 tablespoon of coconut cream on top of the filling.
6. Fold the top of the leaves over the filling. Then fold in the sides of the leaves. Finally, fold the bottom of the leaves over the filling. The palusami should look like a little package. Turn the palusami over to keep the leaves from opening. Then fold the foil closed around the palusami.
7. Repeat steps 4 through 6 with the remaining leaves and filling.
8. Place the foil packages on a baking sheet. Bake them for 30 minutes. To serve, carefully open a foil package and slide the palusami onto a plate.

Finnish Salmon Soup

Salmon soup represents the Finnish respect for nature and natural ingredients. The dish likely dates back hundreds of years.

Ingredients
(makes 8 servings)

- ¼ cup butter
- 1 large onion, chopped
- 1 carrot, peeled and chopped
- 1 celery stalk, chopped
- 3 tablespoons flour
- ½ teaspoon salt
- ½ teaspoon pepper
- 4 cups chicken broth
- 2 cups peeled and cubed potatoes
- two 5-ounce cans boneless, skinless, water-packed salmon, drained
- 1 cup corn kernels, canned or frozen
- 1 cup heavy cream
- fresh parsley for garnish

1. Melt the butter in a pot over medium-high heat. Add the onion, carrots, and celery. Cook until the vegetables begin to soften, stirring often.

2. Sprinkle the flour, salt, and pepper over the vegetables. Stir until well-coated.

3. Pour the chicken broth in a little at a time. Stir constantly to prevent lumps.

4. Add the potatoes, salmon, and corn to the pot. Bring the soup to a boil.

5. Cover the pot and reduce the heat to medium low. Let the soup simmer for 20 to 30 minutes, or until the potatoes are soft.

6. Stir in the heavy cream until it is just warmed. Be careful not to let the soup boil after you've added the cream.

7. Spoon the soup into bowls. Serve it warm with parsley for garnish.

lohikeitto

Salmon is the most commonly eaten fish in Finland. Salmon soup is called *lohikeitto* (loh-he-KAY-toh) in Finnish. *Lohi* means "salmon" and *keitto* means "soup."

Learn Marathi

Marathi (mah-RAH-thee) is the official language of Maharashtra. *Kakadi* (KAH-kah-dee) means "cucumber" in Marathi. *Dhirde* (deer-DAY) means "pancakes."

Indian Cucumber Pancakes

Cucumber pancakes are considered a quick and easy meal in India. They are most popular in the Maharashtra region of west India.

Ingredients
(makes 4 servings)

- 1 cup grated cucumber
- ½ teaspoon salt
- 1 cup rice flour
- ¼ cup shredded spinach
- ¼ cup plain yogurt
- 1 teaspoon chili powder
- ½ teaspoon turmeric powder
- ¾ cup water
- 2 teaspoons vegetable oil
- green chutney (optional, available at most Indian grocery stores)

1. Pat the cucumber dry with paper towels. Toss the cucumber and salt together on a plate. Let the cucumber sit for at least 10 minutes. The salt will help draw water from the cucumber. Then squeeze any remaining water from the cucumber with clean hands.

2. Mix together the cucumber, rice flour, spinach, yogurt, chili powder, and turmeric in a bowl. Stir in the water to make a thick, smooth pancake batter.

3. Heat about ½ teaspoon oil in a pan over medium-high heat.

4. Use a ¼-cup measuring cup to scoop batter into the hot pan. Make two or three pancakes at a time. Cook the pancakes until the edges begin to brown, about 3 minutes. Use a spatula to flip them. Cook for an additional 1 minute.

5. Repeat steps 3 and 4 with the remaining batter.

6. If you'd like, serve the pancakes with green chutney.

Colombian Bocadillo con Queso

In Spanish, *bocadillo* (boh-kah-DEE-oh) means "little snack." In Colombia, bocadillo is a guava candy. It is often served con queso (cohn KAY-soh), or with cheese.

Ingredients
(makes 2 sandwiches)

- 14 ounces guava paste
- 4 thick slices of white bread
- 10 ounces queso fresco
- 2 tablespoons butter

1. Cut two to three thin slices of guava paste. Lay them on one slice of bread.
2. Cut two to three thin slices of queso fresco. Layer them on top of the guava.
3. Place a second slice of bread on top of the queso fresco to complete the sandwich.
4. Melt 1 tablespoon butter in a frying pan over medium heat.
5. Cook the sandwich on one side until golden, about 3 minutes. Flip the sandwich with a spatula and cook for another 3 minutes, or until both sides are golden and the cheese is melting.
6. Repeat steps 1 through 5 to make a second sandwich. Cut the sandwiches in half and serve them warm.

Guava

Guava is called *guayaba* (gway-AH-bah) in Spanish, Colombia's official language. It is one of the country's most popular fruits.

Pierogi Ruskie

In Polish, cheese, potato, and onion pierogi are called *pierogi Ruskie* (pyeh-ROH-ghee ROOS-kyeh). The name references a historical region of Poland called Red Ruthenia.

Polish Pierogi

Pierogi (pyeh-ROH-ghee) have been eaten in Poland since the 1600s. They are served during special occasions.

Ingredients
(makes 2 servings)

- 2 cups instant mashed potato flakes
- 7½ tablespoons unsalted butter
- 1 cup cheddar cheese, shredded
- 2 teaspoons salt
- ½ teaspoon pepper
- 1¾ cups flour
- ½ cup water
- 1 egg
- ½ onion, finely chopped
- sour cream
- parsley

1. Make the potatoes according to the package's directions. Stir in 2 tablespoons butter, cheese, ½ teaspoon salt, and pepper. This is the filling. Set it aside.

2. Mix the flour and 1 teaspoon salt in a bowl. Add the water, egg, and 2½ tablespoons cooled melted butter. Mix into a dough. Knead the dough on a floured surface until smooth, about 5 minutes. Wrap it in plastic and let it rest for 30 minutes.

3. Roll out the dough on a floured surface so it is ⅛ inches (0.3 cm) thick. Cut 3-inch (7.6-cm) circles with a cookie cutter or glass rim.

4. Put 1 tablespoon of potato filling in the middle of each circle. Fold the dough over the filling and pinch the edges closed.

5. Bring a pot of water to a boil. Cook the pierogi in the water until they float to the top. Use a slotted spoon to scoop the pierogi into a bowl.

6. Melt 3 tablespoons butter in a pan over medium heat. Add the onion and ½ teaspoon salt. Cook the onion until it is golden, about 10 minutes.

7. Gently stir the cooked pierogi in with the onion. Serve with sour cream and parsley.

Hawaiian SPAM Musubi

SPAM became popular in Hawaii during World War II. SPAM musubi (moo-SOO-bee) is commonly found in Hawaiian convenience stores and cafes.

Ingredients
(makes 4 servings)

- 1 cup white rice
- 12-ounce can of SPAM or other canned pork luncheon meat
- 4 tablespoons soy sauce
- 1 nori seaweed sheet

1. Cook the rice according to the package's directions. Set it aside.

2. Heat a frying pan over medium-high heat. Cut the SPAM into four slices. Place the slices in the pan. Cook the SPAM until it is crisp and brown, about 2 to 3 minutes on each side.

3. Drizzle 1 tablespoon soy sauce over each SPAM slice. Fry the slices for another 1 minute on each side.

4. Cut the seaweed sheet into four strips.

5. Rinse out the SPAM can and line it with plastic wrap. This will serve as a mold. Put one quarter of the rice in the can. Press it down. Place one SPAM slice on top of the rice and press it down.

6. Carefully remove the SPAM and rice block from the mold by pulling out the plastic wrap. Lay the SPAM side on top of a seaweed strip. The SPAM should be perpendicular to the seaweed.

7. Wrap the seaweed strip over the rice. If needed, dampen the strip with water to help it stick. Flip the musubi so the SPAM is on top.

8. Repeat steps 5 through 7 to make more SPAM musubi.

Japanese Influence
Japanese immigrants have had a strong influence on Hawaiian culture and cooking. *Musubi* means "rice ball" in Japanese. In Hawaiian, "rice" is *laiki* (LYE-kee).

Read More

Borgert-Spaniol, Megan. *Tasty Meals in 15 Minutes or Less.* North Mankato, MN: Capstone, 2024.

Perez, Rossini. *Kids in the Kitchen: 70+ Fun Recipes for Young Chefs to Stir Up!* New York: Rock Point, 2024.

Scherer, Rowena. *A Taste of the World: Celebrating Global Flavors.* Oakland, CA: The Collective Book Studio, 2024.

Internet Sites

Meal Frequency Around the World: What Can We Learn from Other Cultures?
foodandnutrition.org/blogs/stone-soup/meal-frequency-around-world-can-learn-cultures/

What Kids in 14 Countries Around the World Eat for Lunch
globalcitizen.org/en/content/kids-in-14-countries-describe-their-midday-meal/

What School Lunches Look Like Around the World
amieducation.com/news/what-school-lunches-look-like-around-the-world

About the Author

Chelsey Luciow is an artist and creator. She loves reading with kids and believes books are magical. Chelsey lives in Minneapolis with her wife, their son, and their dogs.